ADVENTURES IN THE
ICE AGE

Written by **Linda Bailey**
Illustrated by **Bill Slavin**

Kids Can Press

For Maurice. — L.B.

For those first artists, who felt moved to capture their world in a drawn line. — B.S.

Acknowledgments
The author and illustrator are very grateful to
Dr. David Morrison of the Canadian Museum of Civilization and
Dr. Julian Siggers of the Royal Ontario Museum for their assistance in reviewing
the manuscript and art for accuracy. Both were very generous with their time and help.
Thanks also go, as always, to the wonderful team at Kids Can Press — especially
Valerie Wyatt for her expert editing and Julia Naimska for her careful design.

Text © 2004 Linda Bailey
Illustrations © 2004 Bill Slavin

Kids Can Press acknowledges the financial support of the Government of Ontario, through the
Ontario Media Development Corporation's Ontario Book Initiative; the Ontario Arts Council; the Canada
Council for the Arts; and the Government of Canada, through the BPIDP, for our publishing activity.

Published in Canada by	Published in the U.S. by
Kids Can Press Ltd.	Kids Can Press Ltd.
29 Birch Avenue	2250 Military Road
Toronto, ON M4V 1E2	Tonawanda, NY 14150

www.kidscanpress.com

The artwork in this book was rendered in pen and ink and watercolor.
The text is set in Veljovic Book.

Edited by Valerie Wyatt
Designed by Julia Naimska
Printed and bound in Hong Kong

The hardcover edition of this book is smyth sewn casebound.
The paperback edition of this book is limp sewn with a drawn-on cover.

CM 04 0 9 8 7 6 5 4 3 2 1
CM PA 04 0 9 8 7 6 5 4 3 2 1

National Library of Canada Cataloguing in Publication Data

Bailey, Linda, (date.)
Adventures in the Ice Age / written by Linda Bailey ; illustrated by Bill Slavin.

(Good Times Travel Agency)
Includes index.
ISBN 1-55337-503-3 (bound).   ISBN 1-55337-504-1 (pbk.)

1. Cro-Magnons — Juvenile literature. 2. Glacial epoch — Juvenile literature. I. Slavin, Bill II. Title.
III. Series: Bailey, Linda, (date.) . Good Times Travel Agency.

GN771.B33 2004   j569.9   C2003-906478-6

Kids Can Press is a *l'©r\us*™ Entertainment company

It was the hottest day of the year — maybe even the decade! It was the kind of day you could fry burgers on the sidewalk.

The Binkerton kids — Josh, Emma and their little sister, Libby — had been sitting around all morning, watching the tips of their shoelaces melt. At noon, they headed for the pool. But the pool was a six-block walk away, under a scorching sun. Halfway there, the Binkertons were ready to faint!

Desperate with thirst, they went where they had sworn they would never go again — inside the Good Times Travel Agency. Good Times was an awful place, filthy and fusty and falling apart. The Binkertons knew it was trouble.

But they had no choice …

3

Inside, the air was as still and dry as an old bone. Julian T. Pettigrew, the owner, was taking a break for lunch.

The water Mr. Pettigrew gave them was the same temperature as your bathwater after you've sat in it for half an hour.

... suddenly the Binkertons were far away and long ago and not very hot at all.

JULIAN T. PETTIGREW'S PERSONAL GUIDE TO THE ICE AGE

Looking for a cool vacation? You've come to the right place — Europe 20 000 years ago. Welcome to the Ice Age!

Actually, this is just one of many ice ages. Earth has been going through a series of ice ages followed by warmer periods for millions of years. The ice age you are visiting is the most recent one. It began about 100 000 years ago and ended about 10 000 years ago.

An ice age starts when Earth's temperature drops. So much snow falls that not all of it melts in the summers. The snow builds up and gets compacted into ice. After a while, the ice begins to flow. Eventually, huge sheets of ice cover large parts of the world. In some places, the ice is more than 3 km (2 mi.) thick.

All in all, it's a strange time to visit Europe. Wouldn't you rather come back later? Say, in 10 000 years?

8

PEOPLE OF THE ICE AGE

Hoping to meet some people? It may take a while. The world isn't very crowded during the Ice Age.

Prehistoric people *do* live in this area, though, and you'll run into them sooner or later. The people who live in the late Ice Age are early modern humans (sometimes called Cro-Magnons). They've been around for at least 100 000 years — first in Africa, then spreading around the globe. Clever and inventive, they can adapt to different conditions, including extreme cold. They've been in Ice Age Europe since about 50 000 B.C.

Unfortunately, you're too late to meet the Neanderthals. Pity. They look different from you, with their sloping chins and thick brow ridges.

Neanderthal   Early modern human

Neanderthals used to share this part of the world with early modern humans. But about 35 000 B.C., the humans took over, and the Neanderthals died out.

Before the Neanderthals, there were other kinds of hominids (the family of primate mammals that includes humans), but they're all long gone. The only people alive in the late Ice Age are early modern humans.

9

Fortunately, the woolly rhinoceros had a short attention span.

ANIMALS OF THE ICE AGE

The Ice Age may not be crowded with people, but there are plenty of animals — and some are quite dangerous.

The woolly rhinoceros, for example. BE CAREFUL NOT TO GET TOO CLOSE! Although the rhino may look slow, it can attack with lightning speed. And that front horn is sharp! In winter, the rhino uses it to clear snow to get food. (Think of it as the world's first snow shovel.)

Can you see the woolly rhino's two layers of hair? IF YOU CAN, YOU'RE TOO CLOSE! Many Ice Age animals, including the bison, the musk ox and the mammoth, have thick warm coats to protect them against the cold.

Other animals to watch out for are the cave bear and the cave lion. The cave lion (bigger than an African lion) is the most powerful predator in Ice Age Europe. It eats deer, bison and horses ... and it wouldn't mind a tourist for variety! Its coat changes color — darker in summer and whiter in winter — to blend with its surroundings.

Hint: If you see a cave lion coming, get out of the way. (Too bad you won't see it coming.)

The rhinoceros wasn't the only animal awaiting the Binkertons. Next came a giant deer.

That's a *deer*? They sure grow them big around here.

Those antlers are the size of my bedroom!

Zoo?

MORE ICE AGE ANIMALS

Animals? They're everywhere. Thousands of herds of herbivores (plant-eating animals) wander the northern continents during the Ice Age. You'll like the herbivores! You can relax around them and not worry about getting eaten ... unless you're a clump of grass.

Reindeer are common, and so are aurochs (large, wild ancestors of modern cattle). Another big herbivore is the bison, with its long pointy horns. Even taller is the giant deer, about 2 m (6 ½ feet) high at the shoulder. Its antlers alone can weigh 40 kg (90 lb.). But — here's a surprise! — horses are

And then came a whole herd of bison.

Zoo?

Shush, Libby. This whole place is a zoo!

little guys. In the Ice Age, they're about as tall as an average ten-year-old child.

If you're wondering why there are so many grazing animals, it's simple. This is a great place for them! There are hardly any trees to get in their way and plenty of grasses, mosses and sedges (sharp grasslike plants) to munch on. Most of Ice Age Europe is a vast open grassland called a steppe — perfect for herds of herbivores.

(Ice Age tongue-twister: Say "herds of heavy herbivores" five times as fast as you can. Faster! FASTER!)

13

For the next few hours, the Binkertons wandered, lost and confused, through the Ice Age landscape. They were getting hungrier by the minute.

Wasn't it bad enough to be hungry? Did the Binkertons really need a *new* problem?

Uh-oh. Snow.

Yikes!

Behind the snow came wind ... and a lot more snow ...

Hey, Mr. Pettigrew, you can stop now. This is *cool* enough.

... and something even scarier than the weather.

Now *this* is ... RIDICULOUS!

ICE AGE CLIMATE

Brrrrr! Are you getting cold? Average temperatures in the Ice Age are about 8°C (14°F) colder than in modern times. Even in summer, the warmest it ever gets here is about 10° to 15°C (50° to 60°F), and for some crazy reason, *you* have chosen to arrive at the beginning of winter. (I hope you brought long underwear.)

Cold temperatures aren't the only problem. Have you ever felt such a harsh wind? On these open grasslands, there's not much to stop it, so it howls down, fierce and biting and freezing and ...

No sense boring you with what you already know. The best thing to do is find shelter, especially if it starts to snow. To stay alive in a climate like this, you'll need three things: clothing, shelter and fire. Get busy!

Suddenly out of the storm came a fearful apparition.

Frozen in their tracks by fear, the Binkertons could only stare.

Grraaauuh!

The girl — that's what the Binkertons realized she was — wanted them to follow her.

You're actually going with her?

Got any better ideas?

A short walk later (but long enough to get really, really cold), the Binkertons found themselves in a cave.

Isn't this place missing something? Like a wall?

He doesn't mean it. This is lovely. Really it is!

FIRE

Hit a cold spell? No problem! Build a fire.

Don't know how to build a fire? No problem! Find an early modern human to help you.

The use of fire goes back a long time — hundreds of thousands of years. By the Ice Age, humans have become quite skilled at fire-building. They can start fires by rubbing a stick against a piece of wood to create friction and heat.

They can also strike a flint stone against another stone to make a spark that will drop onto dry material and set it on fire.

In a place like this, with no stoves, furnaces or electricity, fire is extremely important. Besides keeping you warm, it's useful for:
• Providing light.
• Cooking and preserving food.
• Keeping away predators — such as large hungry lions!
• Driving away bugs.
• Shaping and hardening the points of wooden tools.
• Scaring animals into an ambush.
• Sending smoke signals.

Be grateful for your fire and tend it carefully. Do not let it go out ... or that large hungry you-know-what could be back!

19

The girl, whose name was Ula, explained that her real home was a long walk away. She'd been out gathering food, and, like the Binkertons, was caught by the storm.

Dinner that night was extremely simple. But the Binkertons were in no position to be choosy.

The kids — four of them now — settled down for the night, huddling together for warmth.

How come I always get the lumpy bed?

They're all lumpy, Josh. Go to sleep!

FOOD

If you get hungry here in the Ice Age, you have two choices:
1. Hunt.
2. Gather.

Like the people who live here, you will have to become a hunter-gatherer to feed yourself.

Gathering is easy ... or is it? Gathering just means finding leaves, roots, fruit, seeds, nuts and mushrooms that are good to eat. But how will you know which plants are edible and which are (gulp) poisonous?

Ask someone who lives here. Over thousands of years, through trial and error, humans have figured out which plants are good to eat. They have learned where the best plants grow and when they are ready to pick. They use digging sticks to help them harvest the plants. When they get the chance, they gather shellfish, snails and birds' eggs, too.

If you want meat, you'll have to learn to hunt. Hunters here get a lot of reindeer, bison and horse meat. Beginners like you may want to start with rabbits or squirrels. Before you go hunting, though, ask yourself — are you ready for this? There's a lot of blood involved. Some of it may be *yours*!

If you're near water, try fishing instead. It's easier. (Not really.)

Morning dawned bright and sunny, with melting snow. After a breakfast of roots and nuts, the Binkertons followed Ula as she set off for home. Eventually, they reached a river.

Are you hungry? I have —

Yeah, we know. Roots and nuts.

HOMES

Need a place to stay? Look for a nice, cozy cave. The area you're in — southern France — is a favorite spot for prehistoric people. Its limestone cliffs are like honeycombs, full of holes made by water and frost. There are hundreds of natural caves and shelters here, just ready to move into.

Here are a few tips for finding a good one. Choose a cave or shelter that faces south (to get the sun) and with a good overhang (to keep out rain and snow). Try to get a view so you can be the first to see passing herds of animals. Look for a cave with a good-sized opening. That's where you'll live. The deep parts of caves are dark, wet and slippery.

Late that afternoon, they arrived at Ula's home.

Home? It's another cave!

What were you expecting? An apartment building?

If your cave is big enough, you can divide it into living room, bedroom and work room. (Just kidding about the rooms, but you can make dividers out of branches and animal skins.) Having separate areas is a good idea. That way you don't have to sleep on wood chips and bits of rock left over from your toolmaking.

Got your cave ready? Relax. Build a fire at the entrance. Pull up a rock to sit on. There! Cozy.

But wait! What if you're in an area where caves are scarce? The people in the rest of Ice Age Europe make do with whatever they can build. They make frames out of branches or bones and cover them with turf or animal skins — kind of like tents. Imagine living in a tent in this climate! No wonder caves are so popular.

The Binkertons did their best to fit in. They tried to be good guests and make themselves useful.

Oh! I see you're scraping skins to make clothes. Can I help?

It wasn't easy.

Would you happen to have one that's not quite so ... bloody?

Eww! Yuck! Gross!

CLOTHING

Every visitor to the Ice Age needs a set of warm clothing. You'll want pants, shirt, a hat and maybe a cloak with a hood. For your feet, try fur boots or moccasins.

But wait! There are no malls here. If you want clothes, you'll have to make your own. Here's how.

1. Get yourself a dead, furbearing animal. (You could *try* a live one, but it might not cooperate with step 2.)
2. Skin the animal with a chipped stone knife.
3. Scrape the skin to soften it and to remove the meat, fat and blood.
4. Stretch the skin or weigh it down to keep it flat as it dries.
5. Treat the skin by smoking it or rubbing animal brains into it to keep it soft.
6. Cut the skin into shapes and sew the pieces together. Use a pointy bone tool or a bone needle to make the holes. Use animal sinew as thread.
7. Decorate your new clothes! Shells are nice. Or make beads of bone, stone or ivory. Try attaching some teeth, too — animal or human, your choice!

24

Dinner was served around the fire.

The food was tasty, but it wasn't exactly what the Binkertons were used to.

COOKING

Don't worry. You won't have to eat your food raw. At least, not all of it.

Even without a stove, you'll find plenty of ways to cook meat here in the Ice Age. You can barbecue it, or "fry" it on red-hot rocks from the fire. Or you can roast it in a fire pit. Just dig a hole, line it with rocks and build a fire at the bottom. When the fire burns down to coals, set your food on top (wrap it in leaves first) and cover everything with dirt. Later, dig up a delicious hot dinner!

You can boil water, too, and even make soup or porridge. No pot? No problem! Just dig another hole. This time, line it with an animal hide. Pour in some water and throw in a few red-hot stones from the fire. Presto! Boiling water. Add seeds, meat, fish or plants to make ... well ... something porridge-ish or soupy. If it starts to cool down, just throw in more hot rocks.

And what's the best thing of all about prehistoric cooking? No dirty dishes!

The sleeping arrangements were more comfortable than the night before ... but not much.

The tasks were a serious blow to the Binkertons. Josh didn't take it well at all.

NOT FAIR! NOT FAIR! NOT FAIR!

This is *not* helping, Josh.

But a Binkerton never stays down for long.

Okay, I'm done. What's next?

We split up the tasks. I'll follow the hunt. You find this guy named Art, and ...

Me! Me! What about me?

Libby can make friends with a giant.

Goody, goody. A giant!

We'll have to help her.

No kidding!

THREE TASKS

Are you having a good holiday? Seeing the sights? Meeting new people? Excellent!

Now that you've been in the Ice Age for a few days, you're probably ready for a challenge. There's nothing like a difficult task to put some zip in your trip ... unless it's *three* difficult tasks!

Here they are — your Ice Age challenges. Complete them all and finish reading this Guidebook and you're home free!
1. FOLLOW THE HUNT.
2. FIND ART.
3. BEFRIEND A GIANT.

No time like the present to get started. Good luck! (You'll need it.)

Once they had divided up the tasks, the Binkertons tackled them with determination. It was clear from the start that it wouldn't be easy.

Anyone here named Art? You with the flat nose? No? How about you with the ears?

My name is Zok.

SOCIAL LIFE

Here in the Ice Age, people live in groups made up of related family members.

There are plenty of good reasons to live in a group. For one thing, there's safety in numbers. You will have a better chance of protecting yourself against a lion or bear, for example, if you face it in a group. It's also easier to hunt large animals in a group. And groups are good for keeping a fire going. Some people can guard the fire, while others collect firewood. Cooperation is important in hunter-gatherer groups. It gives everyone a better chance to survive.

At certain times of the year, your group might get together with other groups at large gatherings. You might have special ceremonies or go on a really big hunt together. And if you're looking for a husband or wife, a big gathering is an excellent place to find one. (More choice!)

Excuse me, um, sirs. I don't mean to interrupt, but I was wondering if you're thinking about going hunting ... and, er ...

Big! No! Bigger! No! THIS BIG!

TOOLS

Visiting the Ice Age is almost like going camping. But if you forgot your ax and Swiss army knife, don't worry. Just make your own.

Many tools in the Ice Age are made of stone. But you can't use just *any* stone. Get yourself a piece of flint (a hard glassy stone that flakes easily into sharp pieces). Find something to use as a hammer — a soft stone, or a piece of bone or antler. Take your "hammer" and hit it against the flint so that flakes break off and — NO, NOT LIKE THAT! Oh, for heaven's sake.

Ask someone who lives here to help you. Early modern humans can strike many flakes from a single "core" of flint. The flakes can be shaped into all kinds of tools — knives, axes, spearheads, scrapers and so on.

Early modern humans also make tools out of animal bones, tusks, antlers and wood. These lighter materials make excellent fishhooks, harpoon points, spoons, shovels and even needles.

Impressed? You should be. Compared to the people who came before them, early modern humans are practically geniuses at toolmaking. More materials! Better tools! More types of tools!

That evening, everyone made music ... Ice Age style. At first the Binkertons were too discouraged to enjoy it.

Mom? Dad?

We'll never get out of here. I'll spend the rest of my life without underwear.

Then they saw their chance to drop a few hints about their tasks.

A-hunting we will go, a-hunting we will go!

Art, Art, bo bart, banana fanna fo —

MUSIC

As part of your visit to the Ice Age, you may want to join your hosts in a musical evening. The instruments won't be what you're used to, but if you sing loud enough, you won't notice the difference.

Well, okay ... you *will* notice the difference. Instruments are pretty simple here. Try a bone flute. You can make one out of reindeer, bear or bird bones. Hollow it out and make three to seven finger holes. Or maybe you'd prefer a rasp? Make some ridges or grooves in a surface (bone, stone, shell) and scrape it

with a stick. You'll get the same kind of sound you get by scraping a ruler along a fence. You can also beat on large bones to get drumlike sounds or shake rattles made from gourds filled with stones.

Or try "playing" a cave. Look for folds in the rock walls and hit them with a stick or bone. You can make all kinds of weird sounds. Your voice might sound pretty interesting, too, inside a cave.

If all else fails, use your own body to make music. Sing, clap, stomp your feet and — use your imagination!

When the storytelling started, they dropped a few more hints.

And at the top of the bean stalk lived a horrible mean giant!

THIS BIG!

Finally, at the end of the evening, the Binkertons got a lucky break.

Really? You'll take us to Art?

Art? Yes, tomorrow.

Bean stalk?

LANGUAGE

Music is great, but what else can you do at the end of a long hard day in the Ice Age? There's no TV here. No books, computers or board games, either.

Why not join the crowd around the fire and tell a few stories? Early people have likely always communicated by using simple sounds and gestures. But the early modern humans of the Ice Age are probably the first people ever to fully use a spoken language.

What gave them the gift of the gab? Their brains are larger than most earlier peoples, and they are able to have complicated thoughts and ideas. This gives them something to talk about. Also, their throats and mouths are physically like yours, allowing them to make the right sounds for speech.

So find a seat. Enjoy the fire. Join the conversation. If you can think of a few good stories to tell, you'll be a big Ice Age hit.

The next day, Ula led the way to yet another cave. The Binkertons were thrilled. At last, they were going to find Art.

But inside, their smiles faded. This cave was darker and spookier than the others they had seen.

If the Binkertons had known how long and hard a cave journey could be, they would never have taken their first step.

But, once they had started, it was hard to turn back.

On they ventured, through the darkness and the damp ...

33

...to a place that was absolutely SPLENDID AND AMAZING!

Excuse me. Are either of you guys named Art?

ICE AGE ART

Welcome to the world's first art gallery! (One of the first, anyway.) Earlier people made very simple art, but there's never been anything like this. You could put these paintings in the Louvre Museum!

The masterpieces of the Ice Age were painted in southern Europe 10 000 to 35 000 years before you were born. Amazingly, they are often hidden away in deep, secret places — difficult to get to, and not at all where people live. Why? Who knows?

What do Ice Age artists paint? Animals, mostly. Horses and bison are favorite subjects, as well as wild cattle, deer, bears, lions, mammoths and rhinos. You may see fish, birds and reptiles, too, but not many. Paintings of humans are quite rare. The clearest human images are handprints and hand "stencils" (made by the artist spitting paint around a hand placed on the wall). You might also spot strange markings on the walls — zigzags, circles and so on. What do they mean? Who knows?

Josh! Look at the walls! We've found it. ART!

The "canvases" for this art are the walls of limestone caves. When Ice Age artists see a lump in the wall, they might use it to show, say, a bulge in an animal's body. Cave artists paint on ceilings, too, and sometimes make simple ladders and scaffolds to get there. They do all of this without even a flashlight to help them. The only light comes from torches or oil lamps (flat pieces of stone with hollows to hold animal fat), and it gives a strange effect. In the dim, flickering light, the animals almost seem to ... move!

The artists make paints out of ground-up minerals mixed with water, animal fat or spit. The usual colors are black, brown, red, yellow and white. For paintbrushes, the artists use bits of fur, animal-hair brushes or — easiest of all — fingers. The results, as you can see, are amazing.

The Ice Age also has sculptors. They carve delicate bone and ivory figures that will last for tens of thousands of years. Some of these carvings will end up in the museums of the 21st century.

Emma was fascinated! She asked dozens of questions. But the answers were as murky as the corners of the cave.

What does it mean?

It is life.

Life?

Josh, meanwhile, was thinking about the two remaining tasks ...

Follow the hunt. Befriend a giant.

The hunt? The hunt is now.

... and the Binkertons got their next big break.

The hunt is NOW?

They raced out of the cave as quickly as they could splash, squeeze and crawl.

Move! Move! Move!

Faster! Faster!

36

They ran and ran to Ula's home. They ran some more to catch up with the hunt. They even ran *with* the hunt ... until they found out what they were hunting.

It can't be!

Little horses!

They're hunting them ... and they're going to eat them!

HUNTING

Are you *sure* you want to go hunting? All that blood?

Early modern humans are skilled and clever hunters. Reindeer are their number one prey, but they also hunt horses, bison and other mammals. They know the animals' tracks, paths, migration routes and feeding grounds.

Hint: When hunting large animals, it is wise to go in a group. Most prey animals run faster than humans, so humans have to rely on brains and cooperation. One popular group method is the drive. The hunters yell and wave their arms, driving the animals into an ambush — a dead-end valley or a bog or even right over a cliff. Another method is to dig pit-traps where animals walk, hiding the holes with grass and branches.

To finish off the animals, the hunters use spears with points of stone, bone or antler. (These spears work much better than the sharpened sticks of previous people). Early modern humans have also invented a spear-thrower. It acts like a longer arm, allowing hunters to throw spears farther, faster, harder and more safely than before.

Ready? Get your spear and follow the hunt!

Josh did his best to convince the hunters to reconsider ...

Listen, guys, I've got a great idea. It's called a supermarket.

... but once again, nature had the last word.

Uh-oh.

Libby, come on!

Want to feed horses.

The snow fell harder, and the wind began to howl.

But at least the Binkertons were together ... or were they?

For crying out loud! Didn't we already do this?

Libby? Where's Libby?

In the blink of an eye, Libby had disappeared.

We have to find her.

But how?

YELL!

It took the twins a minute to understand what Libby had done.

See? He likes me.

She always makes such weird friends.

Friends? Did you say friends?

When Josh and Emma figured it out, they could have kissed their little sister. In fact, they *did* kiss her.

Libby, you DID it! You made friends with a giant!

You're a genius!

The next thing the Binkertons knew, they were surrounded by Ice Age giants.

WOW!

MAMMOTHS

Here they are — the giants of the Ice Age! Aren't they incredible? The first sight of a mammoth can take a tourist's breath away.

The woolly mammoth, a relative of the elephant, roams the grassy plains of Europe, northern Asia and North America during the Ice Age. It stands 2.75–3.5 m (9–11 ft.) tall and can weigh as much as 6 or 7 t (tn.). If you have any trouble recognizing it (are you kidding?), look for a sloping back, a hump, huge tusks and a hairy coat.

The hairy coat is, of course, very useful in this climate. It has two layers — thick and woolly on the inside and long and stringy on the outside. The trunk, like an elephant's trunk, is really a long nose. But unlike *your* nose, it can be used for eating, drinking, greeting and carrying things — or breaking an enemy's back! Mammoth tusks, like elephant tusks, are really long teeth. They grow all through the mammoth's life, twisting and spiraling.

These tusks are useful for eating, stripping bark, digging up plants and scraping snow away — and are also good for stabbing an enemy!

At least you won't have to worry about being eaten. Mammoths are completely vegetarian. They eat grass mostly, but also leaves, barks and twigs — altogether 135–180 kg (300–400 lb.) of food a day. No wonder they spend almost all their time eating.

Mammoths can be hunted for food — with great difficulty. There are also plenty of mammoth bones and tusks lying around over many parts of Europe, which can be burned for fuel or used to make tools, beads and even homes. Yes, people here make homes out of whatever is handy — including dead mammoths.

Moments later, the mammoths moved on.

WOW!

EXTINCTION

When you go back to your own time — *if* you go back to your own time — you won't see any mammoths. The mammoth, along with many other large Ice Age mammals, became extinct 10 000 to 12 000 years before your time.

Why? No one knows for sure. One theory blames climate change. When the world warmed up after the last ice age, the landscape and vegetation changed, too. Grasslands turned into forests and boggy plains that were less suited to the giants of the Ice Age. The problem with this theory is that there still were *some* grasslands available.

Another idea is that human hunters killed so many mammoths and other large animals that the populations couldn't survive. The problem with this theory is — it's hard to believe. Could hunters with spears really kill that many animals spread out over vast distances?

Most likely, the answer is complicated. It could have involved both climate and human hunters. Unfortunately, the extinction of Ice Age mammals is still a mystery. But if you would care to stick around and find out, you could tell the whole world!

(No pressure. Just think about it, okay?)

The Binkertons were ready to move on, too.

Let's finish reading and go home.

Why is it blurry?

There was just one small problem.

It is blurry! I can hardly read it!

Ohmygosh. We'll be stuck here!

Well, okay. There were actually a *few* small problems.

READ!

My nose hairs are frozen! I can't feel my feet! We're all going to —

DIE?

The Binkertons focused every last shred of concentration they had on the disappearing words. Could ... they ... finish ... reading ... in ... time?

GOOD-BYE TO THE ICE AGE

Thinking about leaving the Ice Age? Perhaps you have completed your three tasks and think that now is the time to depart?

Don't forget that you still have one more task to complete. You must finish reading this book! And that may not be as easy as you think. For example, snow may fall on these pages and melt, blurring the print. Ice may gather on your eyelashes, blurring your vision. Your hands may get too cold to hold this book.

Perhaps you should think about staying here a little longer. After all, you haven't yet solved the mystery of why large animals of the Ice Age became extinct. If you stay, you could find out the answers to other questions scientists ask about early modern humans — about their beliefs and how they get along with one another and raise their children.

Are you sure you wouldn't like to stay? Can you even read these words?

They could! They did! The Binkertons were back in the travel agency, having a complete meltdown.

Oh, there you are! Now what was it you asked for? Ice?

For a moment, they were speechless ... but only a moment.

NO ICE!

THE ICE AGE

Fact or fantasy?

How much can you believe of *Adventures in the Ice Age?* The Binkerton kids are made up. Their adventures are made up, too. So the story of the Binkertons is just that — a story.

But there really was an Ice Age, when mammoths roamed the earth and people painted in caves, and … well, if you really want to know, read the Guidebook! All the information in Julian T. Pettigrew's Personal Guide to the Ice Age is based on scientists' research and their interpretation of how people lived way back then.

More about the Ice Age

The Ice Age described in this book was only one of many in Earth's past. It was a time (100 000 to 10 000 years ago) when ice covered vast portions of Earth. You can see these ice-covered areas on the map. The X marks the spot where the Binkertons visited, in what is now France. This area is rich in cave art and other evidence of Ice Age people.

Perhaps the most interesting thing about this time and place is the early modern humans who lived there. They looked very much like us, and they were astonishingly creative. The Ice Agers of this time invented new tools and technology and produced magnificent art. They probably also told stories and made music and may even have developed a kind of religion.

The word "probably" is important. The early modern humans in this book were prehistoric ("before history") people. They left no written records to tell us about their lives. So we can only guess about them from the things they did leave behind. One of these things was art, both cave paintings and carved objects. They also left other remains now studied by archeologists (people who study life in long-ago times). These include tools, weapons, fire hearths, frameworks of homes, bones of hunted animals — and their own skeletons.

The skeletons of early modern humans provide evidence about their health, life span, body and brain size and even their social relationships and clothing. (Although the clothing itself didn't last, the beads that decorated it did survive. The arrangement of these beads on skeletons give clues about what people wore.)

Still, there's a lot of guesswork, and many questions remain. One of the most intriguing is why early modern humans painted on cave walls. What did these paintings mean? Why were they painted in such difficult-to-reach places? We can only guess … and hope to find more clues.

Scientists never stop searching for new information about the prehistoric past. They would love to time travel to the Ice Age. If only they could find the right travel agency …

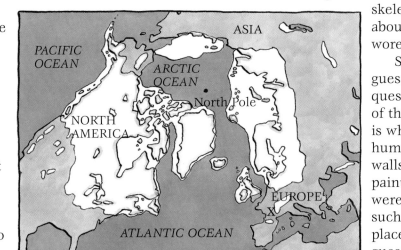

In this book